M000312991

A Map of Love

A Map of Love

M. WYNN THOMAS

Illustrations by Ruth Jên Evans

2023

Text © M. Wynn Thomas, 2023
Illustrations © Ruth Jên Evans, 2023

All rights reserved. No part of this book may
be reproduced in any material form (including
photocopying or storing it in any medium by
electronic means and whether or not transiently or
incidentally to some other use of this publication)
without the written permission of the copyright
owner. Applications for the copyright owner's
written permission to reproduce any part of
this publication should be addressed to the
University of Wales Press, University Registry,
King Edward VII Avenue, Cardiff CF10 3NS.

www.uwp.co.uk

British Library CIP Data

A catalogue record for this book
is available from the British Library.

ISBN: 978-1-915279-43-9
ISBN epub: 978-1-915279-44-6

The right of M. Wynn Thomas to be identified
as author of this work has been asserted in
accordance with sections 77 and 79 of the
Copyright, Designs and Patents Act 1988.

The publisher acknowledges the financial
support of the Books Council of Wales

FSC
www.fsc.org
MIX
Paper | Supporting
responsible forestry
FSC® C013604

Contents

Prefatory Note

Sun Burn
Dafydd ap Gwilym
Morfudd fel yr Haul
page 1

A Closed Door
Llywelyn Goch ap Meurig Hen
Marwnad Lleucu Llwyd
page 9

A Vagina Monologue
Gwerful Mechain
Cywydd y Cedor
page 21

Uncommon Sense
Anon.
untitled
page 31

Macho Men
T. Harri Jones
Love's Mythology
page 39

Erotic Shipwreck
Brenda Chamberlain
untitled
page 45

A Hippopotamus
Bobi Jones
Menyw Feichiog (mewn gwely)
page 49

A Mother's Love
Gillian Clarke
The Sundial
page 59

Love and UFOs
Mihangel Morgan
Anfon Hedbeth Annadnabyddedig yn Llatai
page 65

In the Bonds of Love
Glyn Jones
The Common Path
page 77

An Ogre's Love
R. S. Thomas
In Memoriam: M.E.E.
page 85

Lost
Emyr Humphreys
Marooned
page 93

Acknowledgements
page 99

Prefatory Note

In his volume *The Map of Love*, Dylan Thomas proudly declares that his heart 'has witnesses / In all love's countries'. It is a claim for a poet's powers that is confirmed by the variety of poems on that subject in his volume. He spies the 'cuckoo / Lovers in the dirt of their leafy beds', a typically whimsical snapshot of that state of craziness to which lovers have always been prone. And he associates himself with the 'fishermen of mermen', seeing himself as one who hunts for strange, elusive creatures, inhabitants of the fathomless depths of human passion.

In this present volume, too, love comes in what seems to be a bewilderingly infinite variety of forms, both ordinary and strange, lovely and weird, domesticated, wild and dangerous. It therefore covers a whole spectrum of human experience. Love poems can operate both at room temperature and at fever pitch. And the latter, in particular, seem to exhibit one consistent characteristic – they introduce us to a realm of change, of transformation, of transfiguration; a realm where we often, if not always, find ourselves inescapably estranged from ourselves, for however brief a period; a deeply disconcerting realm where we seem to become 'other'.

It is therefore no wonder that poets intent on exploring the world of passion should so often associate it with the heavingly turbulent sea. When Christopher Marlowe, the great Elizabethan gay poet, wanted to capture his experiences, he did so by narrating, in verse, the Classical story of Leander's heroic but tragic attempt to swim across the Hellespont to his lover, Hero. It is a heterosexual story, but Marlowe turns it into a gay narrative by describing how Neptune, the sea god, becomes so infatuated with the young man's lovely form as he swims that he lovingly and sinuously wraps himself around him and will not let him go; with predictably fatal consequences. That seems to me a perfect expression of the plight of 'beautiful people' the world over today: that beauty, which is their greatest asset, is also their greatest danger. And when another gay poet, the American Hart Crane, wants to map the same underworld of passion four centuries later, he does so by writing a sequence that is entitled 'Voyages', because it is all about the risky venture of abandoning oneself to the doubtful mercies of the sea, of responding to the great inviting and insinuating 'wink of eternity', as Crane describes the eternal movement of the tides.

The Brenda Chamberlain poem in this collection dives into precisely such treacherous depths. And the T. Harri Jones poem follows an analogous tack. It images passion as a dark, fabulous world of transformations, of guises and disguises that are at once magical and bestial. In other words, it images the self as infinitely malleable, as consisting of a menagerie of exotic forms. The carnivalesque parading of these forms has been common practice among humans from the dissolute courts of the Roman emperors, to the Elizabethan age, with its elaborate masques and revels, and right down to the present, with its extravagant Rio Carnival and glut of pop videos featuring one or other of the incarnations of Madonna or Lady Gaga.

Both Chamberlain and Jones were Welsh poets of the twentieth century. And thereby hangs a tale. The twilight of the Middle Ages saw the creation in Wales of a gloriously uninhibited body of love poetry. The poets could work intricate gold filigrees of romantic writing, but they were not afraid of getting down and dirty, producing poems that were magnificently saucy and bawdy. However, as the centuries passed, so chapel blight began to afflict Wales. By the nineteenth century the poetry of love had shrivelled to insipid sentimental lyrics, except when passion was translated into sublimely sensual religious experience. It was only with the twentieth century that the body began once more to put in an appearance – and then, even pregnant women began to receive their due, as Bobi Jones's poem to his 'hippopotamus' wife shows.

This collection does feature one poem – by Gwerful Mechain – that would have been deemed too obscene for publication not so long ago. It also deliberately lowers the temperature in places in order to accommodate such different expressions of love as that of a mother for her child (Gillian Clarke), and even allows for the registering (Glyn Jones) of sympathy for the common plight of all humanity. Because all these ostensible 'outliers' are also authentic poems of love, in their own modest way, as are the love poems of old age, even when all passion is spent.

Robert Frost once remarked that helping a reader to understand a poem was like showing someone a face in a carrot. It was enough just to indicate the nose, the rest would then naturally appear. In this collection I have similarly tried to adopt a very light touch in my commentaries.

I am very grateful to my friend, the distinguished novelist Stevie Davies, for her generous advice and support during the writing of this book.

M. Wynn Thomas

Sun Burn

We are back in the grim time of the Black Death with the first poem, and Owain Glyndŵr's rebellion has yet to be so much as a glint in a warrior's eye. Come summer, unruly members of the colourful, bickering company of bards – a closed shop of professional poets jealously guarding their arcane secrets of word, metre and sound – take to the road, or rather to the scant tracks that cross Wales. Some of these are well-beaten paths to familiar doors; those of the minor gentry (*uchelwyr*) and the great Cistercian houses that for a century have sheltered, fed and watered the licensed bardic vagrants, bereft of court patronage ever since the killing of the last prince of Wales.

The bards have their own distinct pecking order, and 'cock of the walk' is indisputably Dafydd ap Gwilym. He is the Lionel Messi of the word, whose easy, eerie virtuosity baffles ordinary comprehension. Better socially connected than the average, he is proudly able to 'canu ar ei fwyd ei hun' – not for him any demeaning need to 'sing for his supper'. And 'sing' he did. In this period poetry was written not for the page but for performance to a stringed instrument such as a *crwth* or a *telyn*, meaning that it has more in common with modern rap than with printed texts.

A native of Cardiganshire, he enjoys star billing as *Eos Dyfed* ('the Nightingale of south-west Wales'). His social confidence is evident in the chutzpah of his poetry, much like the perfect poise and timing of a top performer. Never composing on the page, he improvises on the hoof, and adjusts his poems in recital to the varying tastes of his fickle listeners. He can set words dancing at will to any tune of his choosing.

DAFYDD AP GWILYM

Morfudd fel yr Haul

fourteenth century

Gorllwyn ydd wyf ddyn geirllaes,
Gorlliw eiry mân marian maes.
Gwŷl, Dduw, mae golau o ddyn,
Goleuach nog ael ewyn.
Goleudon lafarfron liw,
Goleudaer ddyn, gŵyl ydiw.
Gŵyr obryn serch gerdd o'm pen ...

Hyd y llawr, dirfawr derfyn,
Haul a ddaw mal hyloyw ddyn
Yn deg o fewn corff un dydd,
Bugeilies wybr bwygilydd ...
Pell i neb wybod yna,
Pêl yw i Dduw, pa le'dd â.
Ni chaiff llaw yrthiaw wrthi,
Nac ymafael â'i hael hi.
Trannoeth y dyrchaif hefyd,
Ennyn o bell nen y byd.

Nid annhebig, ddig ddogni,
Ymachludd Morfudd â mi.

Morfudd like the sun

I wait for a softly spoken girl,
Sheen of white snow on a pebbly field,
A radiant girl, God knows,
Brighter than spume of foam,
Aglitter with colour like the echoing breast of a wave.
Ablaze with light, yet modest,
She knows how to woo a love song from my lips ...

From far east to west, across the vastness of earth
The sun moves with the dazzle of a girl
Beautifully dressed in the body of day.
It shepherds the sky from horizon to horizon ...
Where God's ball, the sun, goes
Is anyone's guess.
No hand can touch it,
Or grasp so much as its fringe.
But come day, aloft it soars anew,
Distantly setting world's firmament alight ...

Very similar – and cause of my grief –
Is Morfudd's setting out of my sight.

(My translation)

Why does Dafydd, this ingenious maestro of the unexpected, so peacock-proud of his originality, choose to begin with the oldest cliché in the book: the comparison of his beloved to the sun? The cliché was shop-soiled and care-worn long before Dafydd's time. Indeed, a couple of centuries later Shakespeare impatiently mocked it when choosing baldly to declare 'My mistress's eyes are nothing like the sun'. So, what is he up to? Why deal in such debased currency?

Because Dafydd ap Gwilym likes nothing better than to change a sow's ear into a silk purse. What greater challenge could there be for a poet? What greater opportunity to show off his prodigious skills? And so, under his hands, and under our very eyes, a long dead simile erupts into uncontrollable new life. It does so because he looks deeply enough into it to discover its unexplored potentialities. If Morfudd is like the sun, then, like the sun, she is bound on occasion to withdraw behind a cloud, to prove temperamental, unpredictable and fickle. But her reappearance is astounding, paining the eyes of her besotted lover, and nurturing new feelings. Worst of all is the time when, daily, her sunset arrives and she retires to her grumpy husband's house. Yet, if only allowed, she could outdo the sun itself in the constancy of her incomparable light and banish night eternally from the lover's world.

In this case, Dafydd uses the straitjacket of the *cywydd* metre and *cynghanedd* form to convey the fixity of the lover's obsession. From beginning to end, the image of the sun seems to stand still at the very heart of the poem, as Dafydd keeps circling it with manic intensity. It captures the repetitive compulsive disorder that can grip a lover's mind. And the virtuosic trick of beginning a long sequence of lines with the same letter further emphasises the fixity of mind of a poor besotted lover.

Dafydd devoted some eighty poems in total to his love and pursuit of Morfudd, who was probably married to a prominent citizen of Aberystwyth, lampooned (fairly or not) by Dafydd under the nickname of *Y Bwa Bach* ('the Little Humpback') and cast in the role (straight out of central casting) of a feeble, inadequate, jealous husband. Also conventional, yet probably based in fact, was Dafydd's profession of love not only for Morfudd but for Dyddgu, a dark beauty to Morfudd's brightness, and modest, which can scarcely be claimed for the latter. Yet for us, neither can have existence apart from the poetry, which makes them agelessly compelling. Both are vivid creations and creatures of language, the language of love; textual avatars who live on forever, larger even than life.

A Closed Door

There are cultures the world over where professional mourners are employed at funerals. Their role is to ensure that proper public voice and expression are given to a private grief that often leaves the bereaved deprived of words. Even in the United Kingdom today, a figure solemnly dressed in black, elegantly equipped with a cane and with a tall top hat perched on their head, may be seen in some places, walking slowly and with due gravity in front of the hearse that bears the coffin. Obviously surplus to strictly utilitarian requirements, that figure, too, is there solely to ensure that the inner feelings of the silent mourners are satisfactorily registered by being enacted in an appropriate public and symbolic fashion.

It was one of the ritual functions of the professional poets in late medieval Wales to provide exactly such a service. After all, they were renowned for their ability to produce words that were satisfyingly answerable to every manner of human experience. And given the omnipresence of death in an age when the young were almost as likely to be taken as suddenly as the old – and never more so than in the time of our next poet, the resplendently named Llywelyn Goch ap Meurig Hen, who lived during the

Black Death – their gifts as elegists were highly prized. Theirs was the gift of releasing the language of love locked away in the shattering experience of loss. One of the very greatest of such elegies is Llywelyn's to a girl named Lleucu Llwyd ('Lloyd' in English).

Marwnad Lleucu Llwyd

fourteenth century

Y ferch wen o'r dderw brennol,
Arfaeth ddig yw'r fau i'th ôl.
Cain ei llun, cannwyll Wynedd,
Cyd bych o fewn caead bedd,
F'enaid, cyfod i fyny,
Egor y ddaearddor ddu,
Gwrthod wely tywod hir,
A gwrtheb f'wyneb, feinir.
Mae yman, hoedran hydraul,
Uwch dy fedd, huanwedd haul,
Ŵr prudd ei wyneb hebod,
Llywelyn Goch, gloch dy glod ...

Myfi, fun fwyfwy fonedd,
Echdoe a fûm uwch dy fedd
Yn gollwng deigr llideigrbraff
Ar hyd yr wyneb yn rhaff.
Tithau, harddlun y fun fud,
O'r tewbwll ni'm atebud ...

Gwae fi fod arch i'th warchae!
A thŷ main rhof a thi mae,
A chôr eglwys a chreiglen
A phwys o bridd a phais bren.
Gwae'r fi'r ferch wen o Bennal,
Breuddwyd dig, briddo dy dâl!
Clo dur derw, galarchwerw gael,
A daear, deg ei dwyael,
A thromgad ddôr, a thrymgae,
A llawr maes rhof a'r lliw mae,
A chlyd fur, a chlo dur du,
A chlicied; yn iach, Lleucu.

Elegy for Lleucu Llwyd

Fair girl sunk in oaken chest,
I'm furious that you've left me.
Fair of form, Gwynedd's candle,
Though the grave closes over you
Rise up, come to me my darling,
Open the black door of earth,
Abandon the long bed of sand,
And return to meet me, my sweet.
Hovering here, prostrate with grief,
Above your grave, my sun-bright darling,
Awaits a man grief-stricken without you,
Llywelyn Goch, who bells your praise ...

Yesterday, I let tears thick as ropes
Run down my cheeks
But you, mute picture of a fair girl,
From the pit made no reply ...

Woe's me, that a coffin blockades you,
And between us, a house of stone,
Church chancel and stone screen
And earth's weight and gown of wood.
Woe's me, fair Pennal girl,
A nightmare your earthed-up forehead,
Oak's iron lock, bittergrief's grip,
And earth (so lovely your brows),
And heavy door, and heavy clasp,
And field's floor between us,
And snug wall, and hard black lock,
And a bolt – farewell, Lleucu.

(My very free translation;
but with grateful thanks
to Joseph Clancy)

Lleucu Llwyd is a name still radioactive with glamour in Welsh-language culture thanks to the extraordinary poem through which, once upon a time, a special poet sent it on its long journey through the centuries. Such is its enduring penumbra of romance that Dewi Pws, a popular troubadour of late twentieth-century Wales, made it the subject of a lovely song. Lleucu is known to have been a married woman from Merionethshire, and it seems likely that she was also the poet's mistress. If so, then in this case the professional elegist would have actually been writing out of deep personal experience of loss. Certainly, the abrupt opening and the repetition of phrase is suggestive of a mind in shock, numbed into immobility.

The poem is rich with *sangiadau*; the asides that are liable to puzzle and irritate a modern reader. But they can be thought of as the record of a distracted mind, a turbulent consciousness that constantly reacts to loss on multiple levels simultaneously. They have structural importance. They keep the *cywydd* psychologically true to actual experience.

For the most part, Lleucu is evoked by Llywelyn in terms of features and forces from the world of nature – as if her abrupt death had made him painfully and acutely aware anew of the evanescence of life and the frailty of the flesh; as if her dying had heightened his appreciation of the fleeting, sensuous vitality of the surrounding world. Then, in what is no doubt a deliberate contrast, the poem's final powerful section dwells grimly on 'glowing fleshed'

Lleucu's motionless incarceration in an oaken coffin:
a move from the luminous to the dark.

Whereas up until now the poem has been full of the restless vitality of motion ('hue of rivers' ripples), it now turns blankly static as it imagines 'Church chancel and stone screen / And earth's weight and gown of wood'. And implicit in Llywelyn's macabre, remorseless imagining of his separation from Lleucu by 'hard oak's lock, bittergrief's grip … And heavy door, heavy clasp … and hard black lock / and a bolt' are memories of a door that would once have been so willingly opened to admit him. Just as when he beseeches her to 'forsake the long bed of sand', the phrase is ghosted by a reminiscence of the passionately shared bed of their very recent past. Thus, to the conceit of emotional betrayal, Llywelyn adds the conceit of sexual betrayal as well – a conceit that may even be shadowed by his guilty awareness of Lleucu's sexual betrayal of her husband through her adulterous relationship with him.

The poem is richly seamed throughout with pungent epigrams. For anything remotely comparable in English, one would need to look all the way back to the time of John Dryden and Alexander Pope, lamentably near-forgotten masters of English verse. Sadly, therefore, much is unavoidably lost in this English translation, including the almost indecent rawness of expression in places. So Llywelyn at one point calls himself an 'Udfardd', which is rendered in English as 'wailing bard', whereas the original is a startling coinage achieved by the violent compression and nuclear fusion of the verb 'Udo', which is to howl or bay like a wolf, and the noun, 'bardd', meaning poet. Elsewhere the word 'llideigrbraff' occurs, which is actually an astonishingly knotty and tough combination of three totally different words: 'llid' ('angry resentment'), 'deigr' ('tears') and 'praff', a word that is in itself a whole compendium of adjectives. Although all these possible meanings are different, they intertwine to create a marvellous braid of expression: the tears shed for Lleucu are great, big, strong, firm, powerful, sturdy, thick, heavy, abundant, copious. And then, two-thirds of the way through, the poem switches from using the present tense for Lleucu (as if the incredulous Llywelyn cannot begin to reconcile himself to her disappearance) to a stoically resigned past tense.

The poem is, then, unforgettable in its naked confession of anguish. And yet, one disconcerting possibility remains. The possibility that Lleucu is not actually dead: that Llywelyn's composition is a supreme example of the mock-elegy. The form was very popular and commonplace among his fellow poets. It allowed them to keep their hand in, to bury their enemies ahead of time (and it is worth remembering that in days of yore, poets were believed to have such power with words that they could literally do much harm as well as good). It amused friends and challenged rivals. Such poems were trials of verbal strength and an indispensable feature of the bardic game. They performed, when teasingly practised, the important bardic function of male bonding.

But, even if the poem is indeed a mock-elegy – and there is no compelling scholarly reason to believe that it is – it may still be read as an authentic expression of love, an example of Llywelyn choosing to heighten his appreciation of Lleucu's permanently precarious beauty by imagining in anticipation what it would be like to lose her. And in the process, of course, he would have been drawing the depth of his passion to his beloved's attention. Whichever way one chooses to read it, it remains a poignant love poem, and one with power enough for the name 'Lleucu Llwyd' to have continued to resonate in Wales right down to the present century.

A Vagina Monologue

The brethren of the guild of bards were nothing if not proud to strut their stuff by parading their maleness – as is nowhere more evident than in the uber-macho performances of Dafydd ap Gwilym in his poetry. But nowadays it is realised that there were a number of women that were also active in the poetic game, and the one whose work has come down to us is Gwerful Mechain – 'Mechain' being the name of her native district of Powys. While her life is shrouded largely in mystery, she is generally supposed to have lived from roughly 1460 to 1502 and her maiden name was Fychan (modern day 'Vaughan'). She is known to have come from a good family, to have had at least three brothers and a sister, and to have been both a wife and the mother of a daughter named Mawd.

Long discreetly ignored by several generations of prudish scholars, her work has recently begun to receive intensely appreciative attention, expressive as it is, not least in its joltingly frank flaunting of her sexuality, of her fierce and feisty pride in being a woman. This poem of hers may be thought of as the equivalent, in her age, of a vagina monologue, and it is with complete justice

that hers has been hailed as 'one of the boldest voices of medieval European literature' and acclaimed as 'the most accomplished and most combative female poet of medieval Wales'.

Cywydd y Cedor

fifteenth century

Pob rhyw brydydd, dydd dioed,
Mul frwysg, wladaidd rwysg erioed,
Noethi moliant, nis gwarantwyf,
Anfeidrol reiol, yr wyf
Am gerdd merched y gwledydd
A wnaethant heb ffyniant ffydd
Yn anghwbl iawn, ddawn ddiwad,
Ar hyd y dydd, rho Duw Dad.
Moli gwallt, cwnsallt ceinserch,
A phob cyfryw fyw o ferch,
Ac obry moli heb wg
Yr aeliau uwch yr olwg.
Moli hefyd, hyfryd tew,
Foelder dwyfron feddaldew,

A moli gwen, len loywlun,
Dylai barch, a dwylaw bun.
Yna, o brif ddewiniaeth,
Cyn y nos canu a wnaeth,
Duw yn ei rodd a'i oddef,
Diffrwyth wawd o'i dafawd ef.

Gado'r canol heb foliant
A'r plas lle enillir plant,
A'r cedor clyd, hyder claer,
Tynerdeg, cylch twn eurdaer,
Lle carwn i, cywrain iach,
Y cedor dan y cadach.
Corff wyd diball ei allu,
Cwrt difreg o'r bloneg blu.
Llyma 'nghred, teg y cedawr,
Cylch gweflau ymylau mawr,
Cont yno wrth din finffloch,
Dabl y gerdd â'i dwbl o goch,
Ac nid arbed, freisged frig,
Y gloywsaint wŷr eglwysig
Mewn cyfle iawn, ddawn ddifreg,
Myn Beuno, ei deimlo'n deg.
Am hyn o chwaen, gaen gerydd,
Y prydyddion sythion sydd,
Gadewch yn hael, gafael ged,
Gerddau cerddor i gerdded.
Sawden awdl, sidan ydliw,
Sêm fach len ar gont wen wiw,
Lleiniau mewn man ymannerch,
Y llwyn sur, llawn yw o serch,
Fforest falch iawn, ddawn ddifreg,
Ffris ffraill, ffwrwr dwygaill deg,
Pant yw hwy no llwy yn llaw,
Clawdd i ddal cal ddwy ddwylaw.
Trwsglwyn merch, drud annerch dro,
Berth addwyn, Duw'n borth iddo.

Poem to the Vagina

Every poet, drunken fool,
Thinks he's just the king of cool,
(Every one is such a boor,
He makes me sick, I'm so demure),
He always declaims fruitless praise
Of all the girls in his male gaze,
He's at it all day long, by God,
Ignoring the best bit, silly sod:
He praises the hair, gown of fine love,
And all the girl's bits up above,
Even lower down he praises merrily,
The eyes which glance so sexily;
Daring more, he lauds the lovely shape
Of the soft breasts which leave him agape,

And the beauty's arms, bright drape,
Even her perfect hands, do not escape.
Then with his finest magic,
Before night falls (it's tragic)
He pays homage to God's might,
An empty eulogy; it's not quite right:
For he's left the girl's middle unpraised
That place where children are conceived,
The warm bright quim he does not sing,
That tender, plump, pulsating, broken ring,
That's the place I love, the place I bless,
The hidden quim beneath the dress.
You female body, you're strong and fair,
A faultless, fleshy court plumed with hair.

I proclaim that the quim is fine,
Circle of broad-edged lips divine,
A cunt there by a lavish arse,
Table of song with its double in red,
And the churchmen all, the radiant saints,
When they get a chance, they've no restraint,
They never miss their chance to steal,
By St Beuno, to give it a good feel.
So I hope you feel well and truly told off,
All you proud male poets, you dare not scoff,
Let songs to the quim grow and thrive,
Find their due reward and survive,
For it is silky soft, the sultan of an ode,
A little seam, a curtain, on a niche bestowed,
Neat flaps in a place of meeting,
The sour grove, circle of greeting,
Superb forest, faultless gift to squeeze,
Fur for a fine pair of balls, tender frieze,
Dingle deeper than hand or ladle,
Hedge to hold a penis as large as you're able,
A girl's thick glade, it is full of love,
Lovely bush, you are blessed by God above.

(Free translation by Katie Gramich)

From start to finish Gwerful Mechain's poem fronts up to the male domination that her bardic colleagues regarded as their god-given right. She gleefully sets about shredding the cherished conventions of their wimpish love poetry and in the process creates her own different language of love, at the very centre of which is the assertion of female sexual experience and sexual pleasure. Gwerful was the Mae West of her age. It is easy to imagine her in West's role in the film *Myra Breckenridge* where she encounters a tall cowboy. 'Say, how tall are you without your horse?', she asks peering up at him. 'I'm six foot seven, ma'am', he replies. 'Never mind the six foot,' she drawls lazily, 'just tell me about the seven inches.'

In many ways, Gwerful Mechain's is a love poem to her own sex, in both senses of that word. It is also a mocking satire of all the best efforts of her male bardic contemporaries in that genre. She points out to them that real sexual satisfaction can be possible only if both parties learn to include the most earthy and coarse of expressions in the love vocabulary that has hitherto been so pallid and anaemic with romantic effusion. The poem is a defiant comment on the male belief, common in the Middle Ages, that women were governed by their sexual organs, lascivious creatures of unbridled sexual appetite who therefore needed to be carefully policed and controlled. It also satirises the courtly love convention of the day, which treated women as superior, ethereal beings.

Hers is a call for honesty when addressing a woman's needs. After all, she was probably consciously responding to a bardic male-stripper's poetic display of the prowess of his penis – Dafydd ap Gwilym had composed a celebrated poem on that very subject. Her poem is a mocking comment on such arrogant male narcissism. Not that she isn't herself an avid fan of the male organ – elsewhere she sardonically notes that she would prefer to sacrifice a frying pan from her pantry for it any day – but she is determined to have it only on her own terms. At the outset, she deploys her prominent social status to assert her authority over the hapless bards, and thus anticipates and countermands any male insinuation that her poetry is no better than that of the vulgar low-class jongleurs, the wandering entertainers who merely pandered to the coarse tastes of the common multitude. But she also dismantles the opposite image of women common at the time and much favoured in elite circles such as her own; that they were ethereal beings, to be worshipped from afar and wooed with a mixture of worshipful adoration and guile.

The poem changes tone noticeably once it comes to her advertising her genitalia. It turns intimately affectionate and self-caressing. She begins to multiply conceits with a new relish and challenging originality that is testimony to her authentic familiarity with her subject. In this concluding passage she establishes how complex the organ is that she is praising, how many and different are its aspects and functions. It is the source of intense pleasure, certainly, but it is also the very source of human life itself. At this point her text becomes the verbal equivalent of the extraordinarily daring painting to which Courbet gave the title 'The Origin of the World'.

Perhaps most strikingly relevant to us today is the way that she emphasises the loveliness, the sheer beauty of her genitalia, treating them as a precious aspect of her being. Her poem probably originated as one half of a playful exchange between her and a male poet who may also have been her lover. X-rated by Nonconformity for the best part of two centuries, her work has once more joyously exploded into readers' sight and is currently deservedly riding the wave of enlightened concern with the rights of women and demands that their needs and experiences be allowed full and free voice at last.

Uncommon Sense

The three poems included up to this point were all, in their day, very much the product and preserve of the upper stratum of their society. But poetry has never been merely, or indeed primarily, for the elite. It is, after all, as natural as song, with which it shares many features. Poetry is common. Indeed, it is universal. It arises from basic human experience and it satisfies a wide variety of human needs. As entertainment, it is an expression of the human love of playing with sounds, meanings and patterns: riddles, lullabies, nonsense-verse, comic narrative, these and many more of their kind are familiar verse forms across all cultures. And poems also tend to well to the surface from feelings that lie too deep for tears (as a poet famously put it). They erupt spontaneously and irrepressibly at such times. The instinctive response even of modern New Yorkers, hard-bitten and cynical, to the 9/11 disaster was to turn to poetry as the only adequate verbal instrument for capturing and confining the pain: as John Donne wrote long ago, 'For he tames it, that fetters it in verse'.

The following verses are all anonymous compositions that arose from the lives of ordinary people and gave expression to their emotions.

ANON

Penillion Telyn

Blodau'r flwyddyn yw f'anwylyd,
Ebrill, Mai, Mehefin, hefyd;
Llewyrch haul yn twnnu ar gysgod,
A gwenithen y genethod.

•

Dacw f'annwyl siriol seren,
Hon yw blodau plwy Llangeinwen,
Dan ei throed ni phlyg y blewyn
Mwy na'r graig dan droed aderyn.

•

Llawn yw'r môr o swnd a chregyn,
Llawn yw'r wy o wyn a melyn,
Llawn yw'r coed o ddail a blodau,
Llawn o gariad merch wyf innau.

•

Dacw long yn hwylio'n hwylus
Heibio i'r trwyn ac at yr ynys,
Os fy nghariad i sydd ynddi,
Hwyliau sidan glas sydd arni.

•

Da gael gan 'sgyfarnog gael egin mis Mai,
Da gan wiwer gael collen a chnau,
Da gan gwningen gael twll o flaen ci,
F'anwylyd fain olau sy'n orau gen i.

Folk Songs

The whole year's blossoms is my darling –
April, May, June, flowers blooming;
Bringing sun where shadows thicken,
The living wheat-grain of all women.

•

There's my love, Llangeinwen's star,
Her form is where all blossoms are;
No grass-blade bends beneath her stepping
More than the rock beneath the fledgling.

•

Full the tide of sand and sea-shells,
Full of yellow and white are egg-shells,
Full of leaves and flowers is the grove,
Full am I of my girl's love.

•

There beyond that nose of headland
The ship sails on towards the island;
If my darling is aboard her
Blue silk sails I see upon her.

•

The hare loves the shoots that sprout
                    up when it's May,
The squirrel the hazels he hides in his drey,
And I love my darling as, chased by the hound,
The rabbit loves seeing the hole in the ground!

(Translation by Glyn Jones)

For centuries – even for millennia – many in the ruling classes sniffed at this kind of popular poetry of the vulgar herd. But a radical and revolutionary change of attitude occurred in the eighteenth century when the intelligentsia – enlightened by the emergent disciplines of history, sociology and anthropology – began to realise that the ordinary population supplied the backbone of all social and national communities, that their popular poems were important articulations of general feelings and attitudes, and that such poetry was the vital nursery and communicator of distinctive cultural identities. So, from the very dawn of the great Romantic Movement of the later eighteenth century, enthusiasts set about uncovering and preserving the songs of their people, the ephemera, verbal flotsam and jetsam of so many centuries past.

No sooner had this new enthusiasm for the popular cautiously piqued the interest of the tiny sliver of the intelligentsia in Wales than it was seized and crushed by the icy hand of the puritan arm of the Nonconformist establishment. Every hint of the riotous and the bawdy in popular expression was ruthlessly expunged, any suggestion of impropriety, let alone indecency, was erased. Therefore, the little that has come down to us is uniformly asexual at best; anodyne sentiment at worst. Fortunately, however, some lovely poems remain and the verses here are a representative selection of these.

That these poems emerged from a rural society is evident from the imagery they contain. They would, after all, have been sung at country fairs and at *nosweithiau llawen* – the community variety shows held of an evening in country barns, with bales serving as seats and carts as stages. And they would have been accompanied by a harp – indeed, in Welsh they are known simply as *penillion telyn* ('harp verses'). In them can be heard the voice of ordinary, commonplace human experience at its most compelling – the predictability of most of the imagery used is part of their very point. Their purpose in part was to strengthen the bond of community – so important, in those days, for ensuring personal as well as social survival – by giving voice to familiar feelings and experiences. Their art consists of the skilful and attractive repackaging of the expected: they are a miraculous combination of the directness of artless naivety and the subtlety and complexity of well-seasoned general experience. Like proverbs, they are crystallisations of a folk wisdom born of long existential trial and endurance.

Here and there may be found slyly displaced expressions of sensual anticipation – the description of a ship's luscious blue sails, a rabbit aiming for its bolt hole. More often, however, are the 'healthy' insinuations of potential fertility, in the wheat germ, the nutritious egg, the sprouting shoots. After all, countrymen first and foremost expected their wives to be reliable producers of offspring – their future and that of their impoverished community depended entirely on that. But such robust practicality is tempered by tenderness of affection throughout, although reckless passion there is none – not only because of Nonconformist censorship and editorship but also because to encourage

indulgence in such would, after all, have been to place
at risk that spirit of co-operation and mutual trust on
which the stability of a working community depended.
Intemperate passion was a luxury that could not normally
be afforded under such circumstances, although on the
rare occasions that it was manifested, of course, it was
liable to grip the popular imagination just as much as
it does today, giving rise to verses that have not been
allowed to survive in Welsh.

Macho Men

Full-frontal machismo and full-blooded masculinity are exceedingly rare commodities in Welsh poetry. For many centuries that poetry was cowed by Puritanical diatribes against all things sensual. So, the following poem by T. Harri Jones – one of the undeservedly forgotten post-war generation of poets of the 1950s – sounds a welcome, consciously defiant note. But it does so not in a domineering male fashion but with a voice that is passionately warm and with a sensitivity to a partner's needs. It implicitly acknowledges the lack of models in Welsh writing for what it is attempting, because it is full of unmistakeable echoes of the poetry of one of the greatest of love poets from across the Welsh border: John Donne. In that sense, this poem confesses itself to be a cultural import.

Love's Mythology

I have played so many rôles – swan, dolphin, lion –
In covering you, and still you can reduce
Me to this mere outraged despair
Simply at the thought of you lying naked there.

And this, no doubt, is love's mythology
And ours, but I did not want to turn
Your naked truth to words, not even mine,
Even thought from myths poets cannot resign.

Turn for me then upon your naked bed
Warm shoulders waiting for me to declare
I am dolphin, swan, or lion, at command
Of your imperative caressing hand,

And thus we shall outdo mythology
By being nothing but our naked selves.
Think of me as lion or dolphin or as swan
So long as you are what I lie upon.

Throughout his life, Jones, a notorious philanderer, was racked by guilt at his compulsive conduct, of which he knew his sternly Puritanical ancestors would have deeply disapproved. A sense of guilt accordingly haunts all his sensual writing, and he had to go abroad, in both a literal and a metaphorical sense, before he could begin to assuage it. But of that guilt was born an intuitive understanding that the language appropriate for mediating the fabulous world of erotic experience was not that of explicit, four-letter frankness, but rather the corresponding, or answering, language of myth. Appearing to be evasively indirect, that language was in fact the idiom best suited for conveying a core truth: that in the end, all lovemaking involves not only the active participation of the body but also the active participation of the imagination.

All lovemaking, as D. H. Lawrence once observed, actually happens 'in the mind'. Before the flesh can be aroused, the imagination must first be aroused. And the artists and poets of Western civilisation have long realised that the richest vocabulary of the erotic imagination available to them as a creative resource is to be found in the great timeless myths of the ancient, classical world. They provide entry into the enchanted, treacherous, restlessly shape-shifting underworld of sensual experience, profoundly transformative of the quotidian self as it invariably – and sometimes disturbingly – proves to be.

Jones spent all his adult life teaching at a university in distant Newcastle, New South Wales, where one of his Welsh colleagues was the father of Olivia Newton John.

But in imagination he kept returning to his birthplace on a small farm in the wild, bare upland country of mid Wales, and to the simple chapel that had been the lynchpin of that rural community. He resented an exile he regarded as enforced and unwelcome, yet that physical distance he had so reluctantly set between himself and his origins may have been the saving of him as a poet. It allowed him freedom of imaginative experience and of creative expression, releasing him from the grip of what were still, at that time, the repressive norms of Nonconformist society. And it is from this freedom that this frankly 'pagan' poem emerged.

At its centre is a sensitive, courteous acknowledgement of the integrity of his female partner's naked body, out of which comes a corresponding awareness that the very act of turning her into a subject of a poem, of making her into a creature of words, could in itself involve a violation of her separate, distinctive selfhood. This awareness is underlined by his awareness of the imperativeness of her caressing hand – into that word 'imperative' is condensed a recognition that she, too, has urgent claims upon his own body. She is an active rather than a passive partner in the act of making love. She is not a blank, naked canvass on which he can paint his own fanciful picture of desire. Implicit in the text, therefore, is a critique, and ultimately a renunciation, of the male-orientated language of myth.

Erotic Shipwreck

Brenda Chamberlain based the next poem on her feelings during the passage home across the North Sea from Westphalia, the north-western region of Germany, where she had paid a visit to the moated Prussian home of the love of her life, Karl von Laer. There she had reluctantly realised that, happily married as he now was, he could no longer ever be hers. They had first met many years previously when he had come as a very young man to stay with Chamberlain and her then-husband John Petts in their little cottage in Snowdonia. At that time, she and he had gone rock-climbing together, in the process forming an intimate attachment that, in Chamberlain's imagination at least, subsequently matured into a settled passion.

BRENDA CHAMBERLAIN

Your face is painted on the night.
In demon darkness of storm at sea
Your eyes watch over me.
The vessel rolls, tosses, pitches,
Always away from the home of your presence.

O silver school of fish
Through which we thresh:
O salt fathoms, weeds, reefs, O gigantic
Chaos of waters, cover my heart.

I am shipwrecked on the headland of your brow.
My finger has touched your cheek:
You have touched my hand. Now I must drown
In the terrible North Sea, let myself
Be carried helpless, onto the fatal rock.

What is arresting about the poem is its totally uninhibited nature, its startlingly frank confession to a state of hopeless, helpless passion whose very excessiveness, as Chamberlain must have known, rendered it liable to ridicule by readers who, anxious to deny any vulnerability of their own to a like fever of obsession, would be sure to distance themselves by declaring it embarrassing.

The sea was very much Chamberlain's element. She spent long periods living on sea-girt islands, first on Bardsey off the Llŷn peninsula, then on one of the islands off mainland Greece. She recorded her version of life on the former in the classic text *Tide Race*, in which she repeatedly admitted to an addictive identification with seals, those mysterious amphibious animals that she knew to be semi-mythic creatures beloved of lore and legend. For her, the sea was the great solvent of sobriety, measure and reason, the vast realm of passion, inchoate, metamorphic, prodigally fecund yet also ominously dangerous. As such, it was, for her, the womb of her female imagination both as writer and as visual artist. And in this poem it becomes the site of the fatal shipwreck of all her desperate erotic hopes, the sexual nature of which is vividly suggested in that image of 'silver school of fish / Through which we thresh'.

A Hippopotamus

Noted painters in fourteenth-century Florence developed a particular interest in depicting the Virgin Mary when she was heavily pregnant. Such an image was known as a *Madonna del Parto* ('Madonna of Parturition') and it was newly popular at the time, partly perhaps because of a new awareness of the imminent threat of death in the wake of the dreaded Black Death, an epidemic of unparalleled ferocity, which ended up claiming the lives of up to two-thirds of the population of Europe. Feeling threatened, pregnant women therefore turned naturally to the Madonna of Parturition for divine protection and reassurance that the child they were carrying would be born safely.

The acknowledged masterpiece in this genre is that by Piero della Francesca, which was completed sometime between 1450 and 1475. It depicts the Virgin flanked by two angels. She is dressed in her customary blue gown, which is left unlaced and slightly open at the front to reveal the bulge on which the Virgin lightly and protectively has placed her right hand. She stands within a tent, the richly brocaded canopy of which is being held open by two angels to reveal her. Along with the pomegranates – a traditional

emblem of the Passion of Christ – that decorate
the canopy, the tent probably also has a theological
significance. It has been suggested that it might be
an image of the Church. It is worth bearing in mind
that Florentine depiction of the pregnant Virgin when
reading this next poem.

BOBI JONES

Menyw Feichiog

(mewn gwely)

Fel hipopotómos ym mhyllni afon ymdrybaeddi
Rhwng plyg cynfasau, a finnau'n grocodéil pren
Yn d'ymyl. Rwyt ti'n myfyrio tu ôl i'th gwnawd-fwtresi
Yn nwfn arafwch lli, gan droi dy ben uwchben
Gan bwyll o du i du, a soddi unwaith eto
I'r dyfroedd llawn. Diddorol gwylio holl ymdrechion
Cefn pan geisi ddringo o'r afon fel petai'r llaca
O'r gwaelod yn rhwydo traed, a'r dŵr yn gyffion.
Mae llond gwlad ohonot. Dylet ddiboblogi.
Fel mam-ddaear gyda'th gilydd, wedi ei gosod
A'i chwyddiadau erbyn dydd cynhaeaf, mewn
                                    myfyr llydan

Megi gymdeithas glòs ar dy ben dy hun: ynghlo,
Yn fewnblyg ynysig, fe'th ddaliaf yn ymddiddan
Heb geg, heb gyfathrachu â neb gan glustfeinio dro
Ar lais o bell mewn bodolaeth nad yw'n yngan.
Mae byd arall ar bwys: 'rwyt yn ei wybod
Er ei fwyn ei hun, yr un gwahanol, yr heblaw'r hunan
Mewn dwnsiwn cêl a gludi. A'r nef yng ngwaed pob aelod
Mae drwot ti dy ystyr. Mae ynot nod ac amcan
Sydd ar dwf. Cyfrinach dy holl gynnwys di fydd bod —
Bod yn lli llaid amser, hen hipopotómos gariaduslan.

Pregnant Woman

(in bed)

Like a hippopotamus in a river's sultriness you wallow
In a fold of sheets, I a wooden crocodile
Beside you. You meditate behind your flesh-buttresses
Deep in the current's slowness, turning your head above
Cautiously from side to side, and sink once more
Into the full waters. Interesting, to watch all the back's
Efforts when you try to climb from the river,

                              as though the mire
Of the bottom enmeshed your feet, and the water

                                   were stocks.
There's a landful of you. You ought to depopulate.
Like mother-earth with your other, set in place
With its swellings for a day of harvest, in broad

                                   contemplation

You breed a close society all by yourself: I catch you,
Locked away in an island introversion, conversing
Without a mouth, connecting with no-one,
                                    listening intently at times
To a distant voice in an existence that makes no utterance.
Another world is near by: you know it
For its own sake, the separate one, the besides of the self
In a secret dungeon you carry. And the heaven
                                    in the blood of each limb
Is throughout you, your meaning. There is point
                                    and purpose in you
That's in growth. To be will be the secrets of all
                                    your contents –
To be in the flow of time's mud, dear beautiful
                                    old hippopotamus.

                        (Translation by Joseph Clancy)

Bobi Jones was far from being a Catholic believer, and certainly not one who was attracted to any cult of the Virgin. He was nevertheless devoutly religious in his outlook on life. He underwent a conversion to a Calvinistic form of Evangelical Christianity when barely out of his teens, and all his poetry for the rest of his life bore clear signs of his deep belief. This was one of several features that made him seem an odd-ball poet, others being a devotion to the Welsh language (and consequent sensuous delight in its possibilities) that stemmed from his complete mastery of a language that he had begun to learn only as a sixth-former at school, and his adoption of a theory of language that seemed somewhat unorthodox to purists of grammar.

He exploded onto the Welsh scene like an unruly, disruptive *enfant terrible*. Both the boldness and brashness of some of his subjects and his extravagant style of writing were unpalatable to some of his readers. When it first appeared, this poem startled several into prim-lipped disapproval. Particularly shocking to them was the affectionately grotesque opening. However, this perfectly registers his delighted incredulity at the sight before his eyes and the overwhelming gratitude he feels to God for such a totally unexpected gift. Jones and his wife Beti had for years attempted unsuccessfully to conceive a child. The poem is therefore overflowing with his wonder at the miracle of this pregnancy and full of not only a tender love for his wife, but also an intense sensuous infatuation with her that has only been augmented and intensified by this new phase in their relationship.

And just like Henry Moore in his monumental sculptures of the female form, Bobi Jones sees in the lumbering, pregnant Beti the lineaments of an ancient, organic earth mother, a mature goddess of fertility and ultimate source of all human life. She is the very image of recklessly bountiful excess, and this he reflects in the corresponding recklessness of his imagery. To him she seems to have locked out all external distractions, to have concentrated her attention entirely inwards, and to be devotedly listening only to the wordless whisper of new life stirring mysteriously within her. She dwells on the margins of a strange inner world, that of an independent little being wholly other than herself. The role now allotted to her by Providence is simply to exist 'yn lli llaid amser, hen hipopotómus gariaduslan' ('in the flow of time's mud, a perfect old lovable hippopotamus'). The emphasis here is on the antiquity of Beti's condition – it is, after all, as ancient as human life itself. Some of the earliest carvings available to us are of the figure of a mother goddess.

But this is a poem not only about Beti but also about her husband. It is his humble confession to a baffled, thwarted maleness overawed by a condition forever beyond his ken. And it is an intimate revelation of that special, mysterious, even mystical power to nurture new life that is the jealous preserve of the female of the species. But Jones treats the subject with an endearing humour. He revels in a *joie de vivre* both of life and of language. And this is a firework display of a poem that captures his grateful aliveness to the world in all its craziness.

Wit came naturally to him, not least because he thought God himself was witty in the totally unexpected and unpredictable manner of his operations.

Bobi Jones's depiction of the pregnant Beti, then, is every bit as religious in character as is that by Piero della Francesca of the *Madonna del Parto*. Except that, as a radical Evangelical Christian, Jones finds evidence of God's special grace and favour in an ordinary, everyday human condition. For him, every aspect of life is instinct with, and bears testimony to, the omnipresence of God. His is a profoundly modern and democratic view of the experience of pregnancy. And in its warmly affectionate wit and humour, the poem is expressive of Bobi Jones's playful appreciation of the wonders of life.

A Mother's Love

Gillian Clarke was a mother long before she developed into one of contemporary Wales's most distinguished poets. 'The Sundial' was one of the first poems she timidly ventured to publish. It is therefore all the more remarkable that it is so confident and mature in form, timbre and detail. Clarke had enough maternal experience never to sentimentalise childhood, but she was alive both to the fascination of that discrete and distinctive phase in itself, and to its foreshadowing of the adult life that was to come. And this poem captures both these aspects very sensitively.

GILLIAN CLARKE

The Sundial

Owain was ill today. In the night
He was delirious, shouting of lions
In the sleepless heat. Today, dry
And pale, he took a paper circle,
Laid it on the grass which held it
With curling fingers. In the still
Centre he pushed the broken bean
Stick, gathering twelve fragments
Of stone, placed them at measured
Distances. Then he crouched, slightly
Trembling with fever, calculating
The mathematics of sunshine.

He looked up, his eyes dark,
Intelligently adult as though
The wave of fever taught silence
And immobility for the first time.
Here, in his enforced rest, he found
Deliberation, and the slow finger
Of light, quieter than night lions,
More worthy of his concentration.
All day he told the time to me.
All day we felt and watched the sun
Caged in its white diurnal heat,
Pointing at us with its black stick.

The poem traces a rite of passage of which the child is completely unaware, and about which his mother harbours understandingly ambivalent feelings. Those lions conjured up by fever are wild, exciting, untameable creatures, fearful products of an unschooled, and accordingly uninhibited, imagination, rich in potential but also rife with danger. As the sun rises, and that fever abates, so the eyes of the child's mind begin to adjust, to address the world in all its quotidian ordinariness – an ordinariness that nevertheless possesses its own concealed potential for disturbing and disruptive strangeness. So the little boy's transition from the one state to the other is not only the result of the fever slowly burning out of his brain, it is also his adjustment to what Freud called 'the reality principle', a necessary step in growing up. It is also the initial stage in the forming of a mature, adult creative artistic imagination, which will eventually be able to distinguish between fantasy and reality and yet be able to summon the former to enlarge, enrich and illuminate the other.

And of course, it is also an adjustment to a world that is governed by time. The poem is a mother's version of Dylan Thomas's 'Fern Hill', at its centre being the melancholy, sweet awareness of how time is holding the little boy 'green and dying'. In learning to 'tell the time' by making his very own sundial, he is unconsciously beginning to measure out the inexorable progress of his own days. He is thereby submitting to the discipline of adulthood. And by the end, that image of the sun 'caged in its white diurnal heat', is an unmistakeable reference back to those lions that prowled Owain's fevered imagination. Except now, the power of this lion is a real power, to the remorseless exercise of which all human beings are subject. Clarke's poem captures a mother's loving concern to prepare her child for the inevitable experience, heady and dangerous, of growing up.

Love and UFOs

The sending of a *llatai*, that is of a bird as a messenger of love to one's beloved, was a device much favoured by the classical strict-metre poets of the golden age. It served many purposes. It allowed them to emphasise and to respect the socially approved distance that the beloved insisted on keeping from her ardent lover, while in fact circumventing it; and it tacitly implied that their passion was perilously transgressive, since the message usually involved a pressing invitation to an illicit tryst. The wit and ingenuity displayed by Mihangel Morgan in this poem is to co-opt this standard vehicle of heterosexual love for his different, but equally valid, use as a modern gay lover, negotiating the hazardous period of the first onset of AIDS during the 1980s.

Anfon Hedbeth Annadnabyddedig yn Llatai

Un noson oer ddiflas
Aeth Emlyn am dro, diamcan.
Ei feddwl yn helbulus,
Pair o ddryswch y tu ôl i'w dalcen.

Daeth i'r parc ar ddamwain –
Paith o fuchedd
Y nos yn gorwedd yn haen
O gwsg, a'r dre fel y bedd.

Cafodd y tawelwch afael ynddo,
Lledodd y distawrwydd drwyddo
Nes i'r nos ei swyno
A derbyniodd ymweliad o arallfyd –

Iwffo oleuchwim fflachiog!

'Freuddwydflwch' – meddai Em' yn ddisyfyd –
'Daethos yn obeithgerbyd,
Gwibiaist heibio i'r lloer –
Wawlbeiriant – cyn gyflymed
Â syniad – yn saeth drwy'r
Diderfyn a'r Llwybr Llaethog
Ffarweliaist â Gwener
A bwystfilod sarrug
A phlanedau tirion a digysur –

Orflwch adeiniog
Lestr hedegog
Hedbeth annadnabyddedig
'Rwyt ti'n ariannaidd ac euraidd
A'th symud sidanaidd yn ebrwydd

'Iwffo oleuchwim fflachiog –
Cer.' – meddai Emlyn –
'At gariad cyfrinachol fy nghalon
Lle mae e'n byw yn y ddinas
A rho iddo neges –
Mae f'angerdd yn danbaid
Efe yw fy mreuddwyd
Mae e'n llenwi fy meddwl
'Rwy wedi colli f'echel
'Rwy wedi colli fy iechyd
'Rwy'n llewygu mewn nychdod
Wrth feddwl am ei wyneb
'Does neb yn gyffelyb –

'Mae e'n byw mewn rhyw nenlofft
Hen slym bach, er enghraifft,
Mae 'na lawer o beryglon,
Troseddwyr a phlismyn,
Lladron a llofruddion
Yn bygwth y bachgen,
Adfeilion ar gwympo o'i gwmpas,
Puteiniaid a dynion drwgdybus,
Gwyntoedd croesion
Fel ambell i feddwyn
A llanciau ar garlam
A cheir mor gyflym
Gyda gyrwyr diofal
A'r perygl gwaethaf – y bobl grefyddol!

'O hedbeth anhysbys' – 'roedd Emlyn yn erfyn –
'Ehed fel aderyn
Lleuferfad, llong lewyn
Un peth 'rwy'n ei ofyn –
Trosglwydda fy serch i'r annwyl fachgen.'

Sending an Unidentified
Flyingthing as a Llatai

One miserable, cold night
Emlyn went for a stroll, purposeless,
His mind in turmoil,
A cauldron of confusion behind his forehead.

He came to the park, by accident –
A prairie of the night's
Life lying in a layer
Of sleep, and the town like the grave.

The quiet took grip of him,
The silence spread through him,
Until the night charmed him
And he received a visit from the otherworld –

A lightfast flashing UFO!

'Dreambox' – said Em' suddenly –
'You came as a hopevehicle,
You sped past the moon –
Sunmachine – as rapid
As an idea – an arrow through
The Infinite and the Milky Way
You bid farewell to Venus
And surly monsters
And tender comfortless planets.

'Winged superbox
Flying saucer
Unidentified flyingthing
You are silvery and golden
And your silky movements sudden.

'Lightfast flashing UFO –
Go.' – said Emlyn –
'To the secret love of my heart
Where he lives in the city
And give him a message –
My passion is whitehot
He is my dream
He fills my mind
I've been knocked off-balance
I've lost my health
I faint in weakness
When I think of his face
There's no-one like him

'He lives in some attic
A little slum, for example,
There are many dangers,
Criminals and policemen,
Thieves and murderers
Threaten the lad,
Ruins are about to collapse around him
Prostitutes and dubious men,
Veering winds
Like some drunkard
And youngsters racing
And cars so fast
With careless drivers
And the worst danger – the religious ones!

'O UFO' – Emlyn was begging –
'Fly like a bird
Moonboat, cub-boat
Only one thing I ask
Convey my love to my darling boy.'

(My translation)

The whole tone of the poem is set by the title. Into that casual, off-hand coinage 'Flyingthing' ('*Hedbeth*' in Welsh) Morgan packs all his pent-up anger and contempt for the many ages in Wales, culminating in that of a sexually puritanical and intolerant Nonconformity, when any hint of a passionate same-sex relationship was condemned as disgusting and sinful. He hints both at the absence of a word adequate to describe gayness in that culture and at the ingenious subterfuges of language to which gay lovers have had to resort to express their passion.

The Dr Who-like fantasy of space and time travel is an inspired poetic invention, beautifully capturing as it does a gay lover's sense of being an outsider in the eyes of established society, a visitor from some mysterious other world. Its passage past Venus makes it clear that it can have no relation with the goddess of conventional love. It is invoked because no ordinary bird can therefore be fit to act as a *llatai* for a gay lover; only some exotic thing from the remotest reaches of outer space, completely free of the prejudicial gravity of common Welsh earth. It is unidentified because it lacks a name, because it can have no existence in the world of heterosexual relations. And because it would be dangerous for Emlyn to give voice to his true feelings and to any expression of his true self.

It is clear that poor Emlyn has yet to step out of the closet – indeed the super-box-like UFO is a kind of yearning, fantastical, liberated version of that closet. His true self is condemned to be a creature of the night, and an inhabitant of a deserted park that turns into a moral-free zone after dark, where anyone can go, and where anything goes. That Emlyn is unable to admit at first, even to himself, exactly where he is headed and why he is heading there, is neatly suggested by the way that the adjective 'purposeless' is separated from the action that it describes, just as Emlyn refuses to acknowledge, let alone take responsibility for what he is about to do. Throughout the poem he is in denial and in flight from ordinary language. And there is a kind of bitter humour in the way that the poem replicates the convention of *dyfalu*, or riff of similes, that was typical of the traditional love-*cywydd*. But it does so with the same archness and knowingness that characterises Morgan's use of language – some of it deliberately stilted and high-flown – throughout the poem. It is a mockery, a parody of the language of 'conventional', socially sanctioned passion. And there is a touching anxiety for the safety of a fellow gay forced to live incognito in a largely homophobic city environment, in the exaggerated concluding fantasy of the perils of urban life.

The whole poem is a knowingly camp performance. The flamboyant invention throughout of outrageous compounds in Welsh is the verbal equivalent of fluttering ridiculously exaggerated artificial eyelashes. Morgan loved gay icons such as Elizabeth Taylor and Marlene Dietrich precisely because they were so over the top. And part of the witty point of the poem is the way that it unexpectedly succeeds in turning all this theatricality into a deeply affecting disclosure of the plight of gay people even in a supposedly 'enlightened' and 'tolerant' modern society.

In the Bonds of Love

Is this next piece a love poem? Surely not, on first reading. Yet, most certainly yes, on closer consideration. In the old days, the chapel faithful would sometimes sign themselves off with the phase 'Yours, in the bonds of love'. And it is that fundamental bond that Glyn Jones ruefully acknowledges he has broken through a simple failure of fellow feeling. The poem is his act of atonement.

GLYN JONES

The Common Path

On one side the hedge, on the other the brook:
   Each afternoon, I, unnoticed, passed
The middle-aged schoolmistress, grey-haired,
   Gay, loving, who went home along the path.

That spring she walked briskly, carrying her bag
   With the long ledger, the ruler, the catkin twigs,
Two excited little girls from her class
   Chattering around their smiling teacher.

Summer returned, each day then she approached
                           slowly,
   Alone, wholly absorbed, as though in defeat
Between water and hazels, her eyes heedless,
   Her grey face deeply cast down. Could it be
Grief at the great universal agony had begun
   To feed upon her heart – war, imbecility,
Old age, starving, children's deaths, deformities?
   I, free, white, gentile, born neither
Dwarf nor idiot, passed her by, drawing in
   The skirts of my satisfaction, on the other side.

One day, at the last instant of our passing,
  She became, suddenly, aware of me
And as her withdrawn glance met my eyes,
  Her whole face kindled into life, I heard
From large brown eyes a blare of terror, anguished
  Supplication, her cry of doom, death, despair.
And in the warmth of that path's sunshine
  And of my small and manageable success
I felt at once repelled, affronted by her suffering,
  The naked shamelessness of that wild despair.

Troubled, I avoided the common until I heard
  Soon, very soon, the schoolmistress, not from
Any agony of remote and universal suffering
  Or unendurable grief for others, but
Private, middle-aged, rectal cancer, was dead.

What I remember, and in twenty years have
  Never expiated, is that my impatience,
That one glance of my intolerance,
  Rejected her, and so rejected all
The sufferings of wars, imprisonments,
  Deformities, starvation, idiocy, old age –
Because fortune, sunlight, meaningless success,
  Comforted an instant what must not be comforted.

Glyn Jones remained a chapel member all his life – and how his old friend Dylan Thomas would have sniggered and sneered at that. Yet they had started out in the early 1930s as comrades-in-arms, two young swashbuckling *avant garde* writers, bonded fast in the face of a hostile, philistine world. Connoisseurs of language, they set out to amaze with their verbal pyrotechnics. Knowing that, makes this poem – plain in style and determinedly accessible – seem all the more startling and touching. It is itself an act of solidarity with the 'common reader' that is a stylistic enactment of its subject – which is the obligation to acknowledge that we all have a world in common.

Unlike his old friend, Jones was to the end a quiet, mild, kind, humble and self-deprecating man. Again, unlike his friend, he was racked by guilt. He had, he knew, been called to be not only a poet, but an exotic poet, daringly experimental in expression. But that gift condemned him to separation from his fellows, those ordinary members of the proletarian community of his home town, Merthyr, and of the south Wales coalfield, to whose welfare he remained devoted throughout his long life. That guilt, too, lurks there somewhere in the depths of this simple poem.

Unmarried women were a feature of the teaching profession for much of Jones's working life. He entered it during the inter-war period, when so many young women had lost their sweethearts in the carnage of the Western Front. And then there was the law. Down to the Second

World War the law required women to retire from teaching on marriage. So as many of them depended on their salaries to support their dependants – usually elderly parents – there was naturally a reluctance to give up an invaluable source of income.

Given Jones's natural inclinations as an experimental poet, the very simplicity of this poem is disarming, right from the obvious pun in the title – which refers not only to the path over the common, but also to the path that every human inescapably takes through this world. The reference to the parable of the Good Samaritan is likewise transparently and guilelessly obvious. But all this simplicity in the end serves as a foil to a conclusion that is devastatingly complex. Yet it, too, is simply worded because its complexity is not verbal but profoundly moral in character.

Some modern readers might balk at the use of terms such as 'imbecility', 'dwarf' and 'idiot'. But in context they are used sympathetically to register Jones's identification with those whom 'normal' society designate 'abnormal', stigmatising them by the very terms used to describe them. Jones himself was the most compassionate of men. As a young Cardiff schoolteacher, he found himself haunted after visiting the slum areas of inter-war Cardiff; as an older teacher during Second World War, he declared himself a pacifist and duly paid the uncomfortable price. Soon after his marriage he and his wife Doreen agreed not to have children, as they could not bear the thought of bringing a child into such a cruel world as this. And so, this poem registers Glyn Jones's gentle, compassionate love for all poor creatures born to die. It involves a self-indictment. But it also quietly indicts the whole of a humanity prone to flee the spectacle of the world's pain and suffering, and to seek refuge in every manner of entertainment. As the mad old King Lear comes to admit in the extremities of his own suffering when he is face to face with the degrading lives lived by some of his poorest subjects, 'Oh, I have ta'en too little care of this'.

An Ogre's Love

The grim ogre of north Wales. How the English press loved to promote that image of R. S. Thomas. Virtually every article about him was accompanied by a memorable photograph. In it a sour-faced Thomas glowered at the camera, while aggressively leaning towards the viewer out of the upper half of the door in the boulder wall of his little fifteenth-century stone cottage. Of course, such an image did indeed reflect a facet of his character. But there were so many others. Seamus Heaney captured one when he described Thomas as 'the Clint Eastwood of poetry'. Precisely. Thomas, too, was an enigmatic, charismatic loner, a figure prone to materialise suddenly on a distant horizon – a man of notoriously few words. He was a verbal miser: a veritable Scrooge. Any communication from him – and such was rare – came in the form of the briefest of notes, never more than two sentences in length. But it was this parsimony of language that made him such a remarkable poet, as the next poem, so moving in its terseness, demonstrates.

And then there were the skulls … They added a Gothic touch to the image. Those few privileged to step inside Thomas's cottage reported being dumbstruck by

the skulls that seemed strewn around the place. For eager journalists, the skulls seemed clinching proof of the bizarre character of the poet. But, in fact, those skulls belonged not to Thomas but to his wife. As an artist she took a particular interest in the delicate fragile structures of the skulls of the birds and animals whose remains she came across on her wanderings.

In Memoriam: M.E.E.

The rock says: 'Hold hard.'
The fly ignores it.
Here, gone, the raised wings
a rainbow. She, too:
here, gone. I know when,
but where? Eckhart,
you mock me. Between no-
where and anywhere
what difference? Her name
echoes the silence
she and her brush kept.
Immortality, perhaps,
is having one's
name said over
and over? I let
the inscription do it
for me. She explored

all the spectrum
in a fly's wing. The days,
polishing an old
lamp, summon for me
her genie. Others
will come to this stone
where, so timeless
the lichen, so delicate
its brush strokes,
it will be as though
with all the windows wide
to her ashen studio
she is at work for ever.

If Thomas was one of nature's solitaries, so was his wife, who, in old age, seemed a shy, wren-like creature. But hers had been a remarkable life. As a young woman she demonstrated gifts as an artist exceptional enough to win her a prestigious scholarship to complete her studies in Italy. On her return she began to establish a reputation as a promising professional artist sufficient for her to earn money enough to swan around London in an open-top Bentley. But then she grew tired of city life and beat a temporary, strategic retreat to Welsh border-country. There she met a penniless young curate, who was an aspiring poet given to writing rather undistinguished verses. Her marriage to Thomas led to a long life lived both in common and yet apart. Theirs was a parallel existence under a single roof: he had his space and she had hers, where they separately practised their respective arts. And over time some of her gifts – particularly as an acute and astute observer – were absorbed by him.

Mildred Eldridge, known as Elsie to her husband, is known for a large mural that she painted for Gobowen Hospital. But in some ways, she was at her best as a miniaturist. She was, after all, the daughter of a jeweller, and had obviously inherited her craftsman father's skill for detailed work. That reference to 'fine strokes' in the poem is a tribute to her dexterity as a painter of watercolours, a kind of art that needs a touch both sure and sensitive. And the end of the poem returns to the same theme but in a different key, as mention is made of the delicate brushstrokes of the lichen that will come with time to cover the name of this artist who was such a lovingly attentive observer of nature.

Thomas, ever a connoisseur of quietness, appreciates in sad retrospect the 'silence / her brush kept'. But he also suggests that 'her name / Echoes the silence' of her brush. The phrase is typical of him in its subtle depth of paradox – how can 'silence' be 'echoed'? As for the suggestion that her name, too, is silent, that can be accounted for by the fact that Thomas is actually reading it as it is inscribed on her tombstone. And then we notice that in the title of the poem that name is abbreviated to 'M.E.E.', to suggest, perhaps, that Elsie was altogether too retiring and private a person ever to want her full name vulgarly blazoned in public. The letters that follow the 'M' and the 'E' and 'E' are deliberately left unsounded, and so remain forever silent.

Of course, the poem is full of quiet paradoxes of this kind, because at its still heart is a meditation on the mystery of time. It was a subject close to Thomas's heart both as priest and as one who took a keen interest in what the new physics had to say about the extraordinary post-Einsteinian realm of space-time. He also believed that aspects of the astonishing discoveries of physics had been anticipated by such great Christian mystics as the twelfth-century monk Meister Eckhart, who dismissed the conventional and popular view that heaven was a 'place'. It was somewhere, everywhere and nowhere already, Eckhart argued; a spiritual condition not a physical location; a different reality altogether.

Thomas was stunned by the desolation that he felt following his wife's death. He went through a difficult process of introspection and self-doubt and was disturbed and bewildered by the unexpected emotions welling up inside him. Rather like Thomas Hardy, but almost a century later, he really came to appreciate his wife only after he had lost her. And it was out of this guilty, unnerving realisation that poems such as this beautiful, loving elegy came.

As for the conclusion, it is plangent in its expressive compression. Thomas imagines his wife as continuing to work 'in her wide ashen studio'. It is a stunning image of this lifelong artist's grave, combining as it does an echo of the Christian burial service ('ashes to ashes') with an acknowledgement of Elsie's 'devout' dedication to her art, an art that had so consumed her very being while she lived that it was impossible for Thomas to think of her, even in death, in any other way.

Lost

There is a memorable story told about the aged Haydn. When an acquaintance enquired whether 'the music still came', the old man sadly replied, 'Yes, it still comes. But now there is no Joseph Haydn left to record it.' Many an old writer would undoubtedly echo the sentiment, and such, in a way, was the plight of Emyr Humphreys as he approached his hundredth birthday – which is when he scribbled these frail lines on a scrap of paper.

Marooned

Caught without his frame
The room became an ocean
And his life not a voyage
But a sequence of islands he
Could no longer reach and in each
She was the principal inhabitant. There had to be
Many others, communities, thriving regions
But in each case it was she alone
Who looked towards him, even held
Out her hand. He stared long enough
To discern her smile and realise
It was his own in the mirror.

Humphreys is best known as one of the greatest novelists of Wales. But for most of the seven decades or so during which he published more than two dozen novels, scripted innumerable plays and documentaries for television, and wrote many powerful essays and poems, he had relied on his wife, Elinor, for help in turning his virtually indecipherable manuscripts into polished, type-written texts. However, by the time he approached his hundredth birthday, Emyr Humphreys had lost his beloved partner, and this poem gives sad expression to the depth of the loss he had suffered. It was laboriously written in a wavering hand, and has never previously appeared in published form.

It is little more than a fragment, but therein lies its power. Humphreys titled his final collection of poetry – published to celebrate his centenary – *Shards of Light*. And this scrap of a poem, too, is nothing but a shard, a verbal sliver testifying to the enduring power of true love. Emyr and Elinor had been married for some sixty years when she passed away, and so it is little wonder that she remained a permanent fixture in his mind to the end of his days.

As for those 'communities, thriving regions' that Humphreys imagines, in the poem, to exist tantalisingly just out of his reach, they are suggestive of the many-peopled texts of the novels that he is no longer able to write. Humphreys was devoted to Dante's *Divine Comedy* and continued to the very end of his days his practice of reading the text daily both in the original Italian and in a Welsh translation. So it is no surprise to discern the lineaments of Beatrice in his image of Elinor looking towards him and holding out her hand. He was also a cinema buff, so it is fitting that the poem should end with a dissolving 'shot' of Elinor's face turning into his own, as glimpsed in a mirror.

Acknowledgements

The following sources are gratefully acknowledged for the poems reproduced in this volume:

Dafydd ap Gwilym, 'Morfudd fel yr Haul', trans. M. Wynn Thomas.

Llewelyn Goch ap Meurig Hen, 'Marwnad Lleucu Llwyd', trans. M. Wynn Thomas.

Gwerful Mechain, 'Cwydd y Cedor'. English translation originally published in *The Works of Gwerful Mechain*, ed./trans. Katie Gramich. Peterborough, ON: Broadview Press, 2018. Copyright © 2018 Broadview Press. Reproduced with the permission of Broadview Press.

Anon, 'Penillion Telyn', *Hen Benillion* ed. T. H. Parry-Williams (Llandysul: Gwasg Gomer, 1940). Reproduced with permission from Y Lolfa. Trans. Glyn Jones, *The Collected Poems of Glyn Jones* (Cardiff: University of Wales Press, 1996). Published with permission from Literature Wales.

T. Harri Jones, 'Love's Mythology'. *The Collected Poems of T. Harri Jones* (Llandysul: Gwasg Gomer, 1977).

Brenda Chamberlain, Unnamed poem. Reproduced with permission from Reuven Jasser.

Bobi Jones, 'Menyw Feichiog (mewn gwely)'. Reproduced with permission of the Bobi Jones estate, trans. Joseph Clancy, *Bobi Jones, Selected Poems* (Swansea: Christopher Davies Publishers, 1987). Reproduced with permission from the Joseph Clancy estate.

Gillian Clarke, 'The Sundial', p.61. From *Selected Poems* by Gillian Clarke. Published by Picador, 2016. Copyright © Gillian Clarke. Reproduced by permission of the author c/o Rogers, Coleridge & White Ltd., 20 Powis Mews, London W11 1JN.

Mihangel Morgan, 'Anfon Hedbeth Annadnabyddedig yn Llatai', pp.67–72, *Diflaniad fy Fi*. Published by Cyhoeddiadau Barddas, 1988 reproduced with permission.

Glyn Jones, 'The Common Path', *The Collected Poems of Glyn Jones* (Cardiff: University of Wales Press, 1996). Published with permission from Literature Wales.

R. S. Thomas, 'In Memoriam: M. E. E.', *Collected Later Poems 1988–2000* (Hexham: Bloodaxe Books, 2004). Reproduced with permission.

Emyr Humphreys, 'Marooned'. Reproduced with permission of the Emyr Humphreys Estate.